dominate in your area of influence!"

THE FAITH STRATEGY TO CHANGE A NATION

DOC MURPHY

THE FAITH STRATEGY TO CHANGE A NATION

Doc Murphy

Doc Murphy Movements

Plano, Texas

Copyright © 2024 by Doc Murphy.

All rights reserved. No part of this book may be reproduced or transmitted in any form or by any means, electronic or mechanical, including photocopying, recording, or by any information storage and retrieval system, without permission in writing from the copyright owner.

This book was printed in the United States of America.

Doc Murphy Movements
2220 Coit Rd. Ste 480-123
Plano, Tx. 75075

ISBN: 9798339597391

Published by Creative Apostle Everywhere | Everywhere Publishing, Plano, Tx.

For Booking and to order additional copies of this book, contact:

Doc Murphy Movements
pastordocmurphy@gmail.com
www.docmurphy.net

CONTENTS

1. Igniting An Apostolic Movement..……...5

2. Christians in Politics………..….…....11

3. Are You a Player or Fan…..………....19

4. The Faith To Finish…..……………...23

ABOUT THE AUTHOR……………29

PRODUCTS……………………… 30

Chapter One: Igniting an Apostolic Movement

To change a nation, we must ignite an apostolic movement.

*In Mark 16:15, Jesus commands**, "Go into all the world and preach the gospel to every creature.** He who believes and is baptized will be saved; but he who does not believe will be condemned. And these signs will follow those who believe: In My name, they will cast out demons; they will speak with new tongues; they will take up serpents; and if they drink anything deadly, it will by no means hurt them; they will lay hands on the sick, and they will recover."*

*1 Corinthians 1:21 For seeing that in the wisdom of God the world through its wisdom knew not God, it was God's good pleasure **through the foolishness of the preaching to save them that believe.***

*Romans 1:16 For I am not ashamed of **the gospel, because it is the power of God that brings salvation** to everyone who believes: first to the Jew, then to the Gentile.*

The power of the Kingdom's good news still holds, igniting hearts and transforming lives. But in our silence, we're allowing the world to steal the freedom and victory that belongs to the people.

Why should we stand back while the world leads? It's time for the church to rise and reclaim its rightful place—not as a mere alternative, but as the answer. We are the light in the darkness, the voice that brings hope, the force that drives change.

John 1:23 John replied in the words of the prophet Isaiah: **_"I am a voice_** shouting in the wilderness, 'Clear the way for the LORD's coming!'

Colossians 4:3 as you
pray also for us, that God may open to us ***a door for the word, so that we may proclaim the mystery of Christ,*** for which I am in chains. **4** Pray that I may ***declare it clearly,*** as I should.

Ephesians 6:19 Pray also for me, that whenever I ***open my mouth, words may be given me so that I will boldly make known the mystery of the gospel***, 20 for which I am an ambassador in chains. Pray that I may proclaim it fearlessly, as I should.

Now is the time to ***break the silence. Let the world hear the truth***, feel the love, and see the power of the Kingdom at work. This is our moment to lead, to stand up, and to bring the victory that only Christ can provide.

The world is waiting. Will you rise?

This is not just a mission; it's a strategy to take over. We aren't called to blend into the culture or conform to the traditions of men. Our purpose is far greater: we are here to take over.

Romans 12:2 (New Living Translation) ***<u>Don't copy the behavior and customs of this world</u>***, but let God transform you into a new person by changing the way you think. Then you will learn to know God's will for you, which is good and pleasing and perfect.

Consider the story of a pastor who struggled to get his message on the radio in his city because the local stations didn't appreciate the Word of Faith message. Instead of giving up, Dr. Bill Winston advised him to buy a radio station. That's what faith does—it eliminates excuses. There is always a way, and that way is defined by the truth that *"All things are possible with God."*

*Matthew 19:26 Jesus looked at them and said, "With man this is impossible, **<u>but with God all things are possible.</u>***

9 | THE FAITH STRATEGY TO CHANGE A NATION

If we want to see our nation transformed, it will require the power of God working through the Church of Jesus Christ (Ephesians 3:20). This transformation demands faith, authority, and a mindset to dominate every industry. The world will start taking us seriously when they see us consistently living by faith and achieving favorable outcomes. A defeated church cannot reach a defeated nation.

In the middle of the second century, a Christian leader would write to a Roman acquaintance, *"We are in your towns and in your cities; we are in your country; we are in your army and navy; we are in your palaces; we are in the senate; we are more numerous than anyone"* Basically the **Christians were EVERYWHERE and influences everything!**

We're on a daring, God-given mission—*an apostolic assignment to ignite change in every corner of society!*

We're not just preaching; we're infiltrating every sphere of influence with the power of the Kingdom. We are warriors, **who know our divine purpose and sent out like sparks to light up the world.** We don't settle for being spectators; we are equipped to boldly step into our calling, blazing trails in our communities, workplaces, and beyond. ***I want to see Christians EVERYWHERE***—fearlessly carrying the fire of God into every arena!

Chapter Two: The Power of Christians in Politics: Faith in Action for a Better Nation

Throughout history, when Christians rise to positions of influence in government, something remarkable happens. We see the steady heartbeat of faith transform the policies that govern people's lives, and righteousness begins to shift the moral compass of entire nations. It's not just a notion of wishful thinking; it's the tangible impact of believers walking boldly into their calling—where faith meets governance, and values meet leadership.

When Christians step into politics, they bring more than just a set of beliefs. They carry the light of Christ into the heart of decision-making, setting a higher standard for justice, mercy, and truth. Politics is not just about power and position; it is about influence. Imagine a believer standing firm in their faith, refusing to bend under pressure or corruption, and guiding decisions that affect millions. This isn't a dream; it's a responsibility, and many believers have stepped up to answer this call.

Faith on the Frontlines of Government

One of the most powerful examples of Christians impacting politics is the story of William Wilberforce, a British parliamentarian whose deep Christian faith propelled him to lead the charge to abolish the slave trade in the British Empire. Wilberforce didn't view politics as a career—he saw it as a mission field. He understood that his faith wasn't separate from his work in government; it was the driving force behind it. Because of his perseverance, rooted in his love for God and people, slavery was ultimately abolished in the British Empire, changing the course of history.

In the United States, we've witnessed countless Christian leaders who have shaped the moral fiber of the nation. Dr. Martin Luther King Jr. didn't just lead a civil rights movement; he led a faith movement grounded in biblical principles of justice and love. As a Christian preacher, his vision for a racially equal America was rooted in his unwavering belief in the God-given dignity of every person.

On a broader scale, we've seen Christian senators, congressmen, governors, and judges bring a Christ-centered perspective to their roles. Mike Pence, the 48th Vice President of the United States, famously declared, "I'm a Christian, a conservative, and a Republican—in that order." His decisions were shaped by biblical values, influencing everything from pro-life policies to religious freedom initiatives.

The Intersection of Faith and Leadership

When Christians take their faith into the marketplace or government, they bring with them the fruit of the Spirit—love, joy, peace, patience, kindness, goodness, faithfulness, gentleness, and self-control (Galatians 5:22-23). Can you imagine a government office operating under these virtues? A nation where policies are written not with greed, ungodliness, or division in mind, but with peace and justice as the goal? It's possible when the people who make decisions do so with the heart of God.

Faith in the public square isn't just a private matter; it's a public responsibility. ***Proverbs 29:2 tells us, "When the righteous thrive, the people rejoice; when the wicked rule, the people groan."*** Our nation groans under injustice, corruption, and moral decay because the righteous often remain silent or stay away from spheres of influence. But when we, as believers, step into these spaces, we become the salt and light that Jesus called us to be (Matthew

5:13-16). Our presence in government and politics can bring healing, restoration, and hope.

Changing the Course of a Nation

The influence of Christians in leadership has led to profound changes across the world. Consider Daniel in the Bible—serving in the courts of Babylon. Despite living in a pagan society, Daniel's faith never wavered, and because of his steadfastness, he found favor with kings and influenced the entire kingdom. His wisdom, rooted in his relationship with God, led to decisions that benefited the people of Babylon.

In modern times, Christians in the marketplace and government have a unique opportunity to lead with integrity. In times of crisis—whether financial, political, or moral—believers can offer wisdom that surpasses human understanding. It's not about imposing faith on others but about leading by example, showing what true servant leadership looks like.

As Christians, we are called to be good stewards not only of our resources but of the authority entrusted to us. This includes the governing bodies that shape our nations. Christians in political roles—whether at local, state, or national levels—can enact laws that protect the vulnerable, promote justice, and allow freedom for the gospel to flourish.

Faith that Builds a Better Nation

The landscape of politics often feels divisive and chaotic. Yet, when believers enter this arena with a Kingdom mindset, it transforms the conversation. Imagine a senator who refuses to engage in partisan bickering but instead brings a spirit of unity, seeking the welfare of the nation above personal gain. Imagine a mayor whose first instinct is not to amass power but to serve their city with humility, righteousness, and vision. That's the impact of Christ-centered leadership.

Our nation doesn't just need competent leaders; it needs godly ones. It needs men and women who understand that the ultimate authority rests not in human systems but in the hands of the Creator. As Christians in politics, we are called to be stewards of that truth, shaping our government not according to the shifting sands of culture but according to the unchanging Word of God.

As you consider the role of faith in politics, remember this: being involved in the government is not just a political action—it's a Kingdom mandate. God calls us to care about the laws that govern His people. We cannot shy away from this responsibility. When Christians step into government roles, they have the chance to align the nation with God's principles, ensuring that the land thrives in righteousness, justice, and peace.

The world needs more Daniels, Wilberforces, and Kings—men and women of faith willing to lead with courage and conviction. As believers, our place in government and politics is not optional. It is essential. Because when the righteous rise, the people rejoice.

It's time for Christians to step forward. **Our faith doesn't belong just within the walls of the church—it belongs in the boardrooms, the courtrooms, and the halls of Congress**. It belongs anywhere decisions are made that affect the lives of others. When we bring faith into politics, we bring God's heart into the future of our nation. And that, my friends, is how we build a better nation.

Chapter Three: Are You a Player or a Fan?

In the kingdom of God, Jesus gave the church incredible gifts—apostles, prophets, evangelists, pastors, and teachers (Ephesians 4:11). These gifts weren't just handed out to be admired from a distance. Their mission is clear: to equip God's people for the *work* of ministry and to build up the body of Christ (v.12). It's a call to action, a divine invitation for every believer to grow, to serve, and to work in His kingdom. There's a harvest to bring in, but it takes laborers who are willing to step into the field and put in the effort.

Just as Jesus walked from city to city, village to village, teaching, preaching, and healing every disease, His heart was moved by the crowds—they were harassed and helpless, like sheep without a shepherd (Matthew 9:35-36). He saw the need for more workers in the field and urged His apostles, "The harvest is plentiful, but the laborers are few. Pray earnestly to the Lord of the harvest to send laborers into His harvest" (vv. 37-38).

In the church, there are two types of people: players and spectators.

Players are the ones who get involved, the saints who embrace the work of ministry. They are active in their calling, driven by a passion to see the Kingdom advance.

Spectators, on the other hand, are those who watch from the sidelines. They're part of the crowd but not part of the action. The 80/20 rule often applies—20% of people do 80% of the work, while 80% sit back, offering opinions but never stepping up to help the team win.

But here's the challenge: *Are you a player or just a fan?*

In God's Kingdom, we are called to be both. Yes, I'm a fan of what God is doing. I cheer for others, encourage them, and celebrate the victories—but I refuse to stay in the stands. I'm also a player, actively running my race, fulfilling my purpose. I've got an assignment, and by the grace of God and my faith, I will finish it with joy!

Too many believers are content being just fans. They are good people, great encouragers, and might even give and bring others to the game. But when it comes to playing? They shy away. They don't want to train, serve, witness, or pursue their God-given purpose. They remain in the comfort of the stands, unaware that the world is waiting for them to step into their role, to take their position on the field, and fulfill their assignment.

Just as in sports, each player has a unique role. If you're a linebacker, don't try to do the quarterback's job. Know your position, understand your purpose, and serve your generation with it. The team needs you—your faith, your obedience, and your willingness to get in the game.

When you're a player, you gain a deeper understanding of the game. You begin to see the wisdom in the coach's decisions because you're invested. You're no longer shouting from the stands, thinking you know better. Funny how the loudest opinions often come from those who've never suited up, right? They criticize the coach's choices, tell the players what to do, but never step foot on the field themselves.

It's time to change that. Step out of the stands, suit up, and make a difference. God is calling you to more than just being a fan—He's calling you to play, to build, and to be part of the greatest mission on earth. Let's finish our race, fulfill our purpose, and bring in the harvest together!

Chapter Four: The Faith to Finish

"If you're not accomplishing anything you are not focused". – Doc Murphy

A Finishing Mentality

This nation needs Christians in their lane like never before. I believe getting people saved and discipled is the key to changing a nation! But, we need bold Believers who know their assignments and will never stop until they reach the finish line. It's going to take faith, patience, focus, and a finishing mentality.

<u>Focused Christians are not striving to compete</u>—they are driven to ***finish.*** Jesus finished. Paul finished. Peter finished. They understood that their ultimate goal wasn't about outperforming others; it was about **completing** the work that God had set before them.

Paul's words in 2 Timothy 4:7 resonate with that clarity of purpose: *"I have fought the good fight, **I have finished** the race, I have remained faithful."* (KJV: *"I have finished my course, I have kept the faith."*) Paul wasn't concerned about the length of the journey; his focus was on completing his God-given mission with faithfulness and diligence.

In Acts 20:24, Paul reiterates this mindset: *"I consider my life worth nothing to me; my only aim is **to finish the race and complete the task the Lord Jesus has given me**—the task of testifying to the good news of God's grace."* He knew that nothing in this world held greater value than finishing the course God had laid out for him.

Even Jesus, as He hung on the cross, declared, ***"It is finished."*** (John 19:30). In that moment, He completed His purpose on earth, having fulfilled the will of the Father.

And just like a runner who knows where the finish line is, we too must recognize that God will let us know when our time is up. Paul expressed this certainty in 2 Timothy 4:6: *"For I am already being poured out like a drink offering, **_and the time for my departure is near._**"* He knew his race was almost over, but he didn't stop until he finished.

How to Run: The Keys to Finishing

In 1 Corinthians 9:24-26, Paul uses the metaphor of a race to emphasize how we should approach our journey: *"Do you not know that in a race all the runners run, but only one receives the prize? Run in such a way as to take the prize."* This isn't about being competitive for the sake of glory; it's about running with focus and intention.

To finish, we need:

- **Discipline**: *"Everyone who competes in the games trains with* *strict discipline. They do it for a crown that will not last, but we do it for a crown that will last forever."* (1 Corinthians 9:25). Operating in excellence requires a mindset of discipline—being organized, maintaining focus, and continually honing the skills necessary to complete the mission.

- **Purpose**: *"I do not run aimlessly; I do not fight like a boxer beating the air."* (1 Corinthians 9:26). Every step of our journey should be purposeful, driven by the assignment God has given us. Set clear goals, pursue short-term missions, and keep your eyes fixed on the finish line.

The Spirit of Faith: Finishing with Joy

To finish the course God has for you, you must embrace a spirit of faith. God doesn't just want you to start well—He wants you to *finish* strong, keeping the faith and serving your generation according to His will.

David serves as a powerful example of this in Acts 13:36: *"Now when David had **served God's purpose in his own generation**, he fell asleep."* David completed his God-given mission, fulfilling His purpose in his generation. Similarly, we are called to finish with joy, as Paul described in Acts 20:24**: *"I consider my life worth nothing to me; my only aim is to finish the race*** *and complete the task the Lord Jesus has given me—the task of testifying to the good news of God's grace."*

What we face along the way—whether it's **hardship, opposition, or sickness—doesn't define when we're finished**. *God* is the one who determines that. He is the one who gives us the strength and grace to press on, and He is the one who will let us know when our course is complete. Your job is to keep going by faith!

So, run with focus, run with discipline, and run with the assurance that the same God who began a good work in you will carry it through to completion. Keep your eyes on the finish line, and finish with faith, joy, and purpose!

Phil 1:6 And I am sure of this, that he who began a good work in you will bring it to completion at the day of Jesus Christ.

About the Author

Doc Murphy travels teaching the Word of Faith. He plants churches everywhere.

He is also the founder of Doc Murphy Ministries/ The Everywhere Network a church planting organization. He is the author of several books and is an accomplished songwriter and music producer. For more information, log on to our website at www.docmurphy.net.

Other Books and Products by Doc Murphy

YOU Success

Favor IS Fair

Frequency

Transition

Eagle Living

Non-Negotiables

Five + One Series

S. I. Supernatural Intelligence

Dream Responsibly

The God of Increase

History Makers

Faith

Born for this

Understanding and Discovering the Y in U

The Apostolic Church

Everywhere

Multi-site Explained

Small Church, Large Church

Prayer Protocols

History Makers

Worship

Kingdompreneur

You are Exceptional

On A Mission

Go Ready Set!

Full Time Believing

Pioneer Leaders

How to get God to Hear You

DOCtrine: The Education of Peace Instrumental Album

Faithfull EP by Doc and Mary Murphy

King Album by Everywhere Worship

Small Church Worship by Everywhere Worship

Order these products @ amazon.com

The S.I. Supernatural Intelligence Book + Song Combo

Order the Book at
www.docmurphy.net

Stream the Song on Everywhere + or other Digital Streaming Platforms

35 | THE FAITH STRATEGY TO CHANGE A NATION

Made in the USA
Columbia, SC
19 November 2024